The Gift of Glossophobia

The Gift of Glossophobia

Poems by

Mary Louise Kiernan

Cover design by Shay Culligan

Cover photograph by Michael Nelson

ISBN: 978-1-952326-92-9

Cover photo story: The black-and-white photograph, held by the poet, was taken and saved by her parents James and Erna. Mary Louise Kiernan's poem "The Waltz of the Flowers" memorializes that day's recital dance, performed to a solo piano rendition of Tchaikovsky's "Flower Waltz" from The Nutcracker Suite."

Kelsay Books
502 South 1040 East, A-119
American Fork, Utah, 84003

You'll never plow a field by turning it over in your mind.

—Irish proverb taped to my Austrian mother's cupboard

Acknowledgments

Without the generous guiding hand of Molly Peacock, most likely "The Gift of Glossophobia" would not be in your hands at this moment. To open in 2021, The Molly Peacock Secret Poetry Room recreates a hidden room that she discovered in the heart of Bartle Library as a student in the 1960s. I invite you to learn more at the Binghamton.edu website.

Mary Makofske, my mentor and former professor, deserves more appreciation than I can ever express. An award-winning poet, she has been a role model for her writing as well as for her commitment to securing a more sustainable world.

I am grateful especially to professor and poet Barry Goldensohn for his encouragement to work towards a full-length collection.

Special thanks to: the English Department at Queensborough Community College; Tempe Library librarians Jill Brenner and Rolf Brown, along with poetry prize judges from Arizona State University's Department of English: Andrea Janelle Dickens, Rosemarie Dombrowski, Patricia Murphy, Ryan Holden, Kelly Nelson; Changing Hands Poetry Roundtable; Cornwall Writers Circle; Hudson Valley Writers Center; New York State Writers Institute; 9 Bridges Meetup; Tempe Writers Forum; and Writer's Relief.

Thank you to publisher Karen Kelsay and the Kelsay Books staff.

My sincerest gratitude to fellow poets Steve Otlowski and Donna Reis, as well as life guides Rich Hotaling, James Gerald "Jerry" Croghan, and Laura Nizewitz.

I humbly offer "The Gift of Glossophobia" to the family, friends, and loves who made this life's work what it will be.

In addition, grateful acknowledgment is made to the editors of the following publications where these poems or versions of these poems first appeared or will appear:

Artspace: "The Trouble with Troubadours"
The Broad River Review: "La Seduzione"
Chronogram: "Mappa Mundi Echoes," "Under the Overpass"
Common Ground Review: "The Un-Wedding"
The Delmarva Review: "Aglow," "No Act of Contrition,"
    "Independence Day 1976," "Stick with the Feeling,"
    "Waltz of the Flowers"
Evening Street Press: "My Free Spirit Vacation"
The Greensboro Review: "Parlay"
Hudson Valley Echoes: "Riptide," previously published under the
    title "Position Precarious"
Inscape: "My American Star Quilt"
The New York Times: "The Triangle"
Pudding: "Thirty-Odd Degrees"
Sanskrit Literary-Arts Magazine: "My Silenced Spring"
Whistling Shade: "Might I Ever Receive a Rose Again..."

Honors:

Arizona State University / Tempe Library 2015 Poetry Prize
    awarded for "No Dwelling."

The Walt Whitman Award for Excellence in Creative Writing
    conferred by Queensborough Community College.

Contents

III. Glossophobia

Prose unfolds time. Poetry stops time.

—Molly Peacock

Poetry is the liquid voice that can wear through stone.

—Adrienne Rich

I.

Love [Slash] Anti-Love

Walk on air against your better judgement.

—Seamus Heaney

Stick with the Feeling

What hindsight can be seen
in a tilted rearview mirror
choked by Mardi Gras beads
and blocked by red fuzzy dice?

Deep in slop, magnesium wheels
spin, spin, spin. The couple,
frantic for a Chilton manual,
take turns at the steering wheel
laced with imitation leather.

Climbing out the window
to hurl mud at his hot rod,
he curses its maker then kicks
dents into the sinking body.

No motorhead herself, she
knows this engine is blown.
Gagged by the smoke
of hot rubber and burnt oil,
she detaches as if watching
a B-rated drive-in movie.

Sideswiped by a wad of ooze
aimed at no one particular,
she maps out her escape route
as the radio speakers crackle
what once was their song.

Aglow

Not

Jimi Hendrix

in white bells high on

stage at Randall's Island,

Joe Cocker in his tight tee-shirt

at the New York State Pavilion, or

Cream in their curtained White Room

could hold a match to raven-haired Grace Slick

the night she rocked on the edge at Fillmore East—huge

with child & aglow in a pearl-white dress cut on a diagonal

with long silky-looking fringe pulsing to the surreal swirls of

Joshua's psychedelic light show—moving even an innocent virginal

seventeen-year-old to lust for a body…some body…any body…to love.

Might I Ever Receive a Rose Again...

I would snap its neck,
let the head dangle
by a shred, then
crush
each
petal,
prick my fingers
with its thorns,
and blame my pain
on you.

Never to Be Titled

I
patch and mend
threadbare fabric
patch and mend
until I perceive
I have stitched
my fingers together
patch and mend
leaving
shredded gauze
and a bloody mess.

Double Vision

Your vision will become clear only when you can look into your own heart.
Who looks outside, dreams; who looks inside, awakes.

—Carl Jung

This dawn, a feverish fog smothers a ridge of hemlock
where an amplified *caw caw caw* rebounds as
the Marcy-South power line momentarily vaporizes.

Not one but two horizons of ghostly gray clouds
blur like a charcoal sketch carelessly smeared—
a beloved drawing now a wasted scrap.

Like a rusty crown of sweat, dew collects along
the twisted pasture fence where crystal drops slip
from diamond barbs and spiral to earth.

Liquid lies pierce my own haze, burning away
my coveted double vision with which, before
this day is done, clarity will have to have its way.

Savasana

Dead Man's Pose

She breathes. White light crosses her forehead,
caresses her shoulders, and fills her chest—
where her battered heart beats against
the regurgitation of the bile in his sarcasm:
It's a joy to live in this house.

She focuses. Could it be he rails not at this home
but at his boyhood house? She holds the breath,
maintaining corpse position as he stands akimbo,
assuming his familiar fight stance.

She rises. From this pose of deep meditation,
committed to stillness, settled on peace, seeking nirvana,
forcing a breath in, she intends that one new day:
It will be a joy to live in her house.

The Un-Wedding

Around the memorial park pond, along
sunset's edge, weeping willows hang
like heavy drapes framing a painted backdrop.
Upon a worn wooden table sits a wicker basket
from which the *Once-upon-a-Time* bride
unrolls a lace tablecloth (Something old),
uncorks chilled champagne (Something new),
arranges diamond flute glasses (Something borrowed),
and embraces a pair of guests (Just as blue)—
a dishonored maid, one lone bested man.
Murmur of toasts, the clink of crystal,
a pulling at the drawstring pouch
harboring a braided band of gold,
its Florentine finish etched with a flat graver—
the same steel tool used to engrave headstones.
Reenacting her unwitting walk down the aisle,
the unveiled one steps to the edge of the dock.
The two witnesses follow, halt, then huddle
to shield themselves within the dark tableau
silhouetted against day's dying light.
Her back to the pitchy water, she pauses—
as if to toss a bouquet to bridesmaids
poised on a polished dance floor—
then unceremoniously hurls the ring
over her head in a single sweeping arc.

No Dwelling

My high-on-the-hill home must be multiply listed
with no time to rue. I resolve myself like
the persistent sparrow mourning its egg-filled nest
knocked from above the front door cornice.
Bewildered, the bird shuddered mid-air,
its wings backpedalling furiously in place.
How fast can a bird's heart beat before bursting?

Quelling my own palpitations, I will mirror
the ways of the winged one that rebuilt its nest
flight after flight after flight after flight,
meshing leaves and twigs with mossy mud, then
weaving in a single strand of my child's hair
loosened during a porchside hairbrushing.
How fast can my own heart beat before soaring?

Mappa Mundi Echoes

Underground
in the abandoned
Widow Jane Mine,
a jazzman
in a porkpie hat
ambles on stage
between lime pillars
chiseled like blocks
of bittersweet chocolate.
From thick-wicked
vanilla candles,
flames flicker
along the gully wall
while creamy fresh notes flow
from the bell of his soprano sax.
The room of rock claimed,
the goateed player slowly
closes his eyes and airily
caresses his lips over and
around that lucky mouthpiece.

Under the Overpass

under the overpass
(vow spray painted by one vandal lovestruck)

i carry your heart

a line from e.e. cummings
the poet and rule breaker(known to spurn
the period and br/eak up with capitals)

who young women came up to(on streets of New York)
to offer bouquets of flowers;be my darling and carry my heart;
for   you   I   will   b   r   e   a   k
                  all the rules
against the concrete pillar one day
below therumblingoftraffic from the overpass
the graffitied love note is ROLLER PAINTED over;

this smitten driver obsesses obsesses obsesses
questioning did lovers ~~erase the words~~
or
did a god hand of government prevail?
[exhausts blow by so who can see what isn't there anymore]

Oh(time passes)
tonight[under the overpass]headlights flare
the stars plunge through a dark called night—
(the concrete pillar reflects) a fresh pairing of words beams

:   carry on

24

Garudasana

The Eagle Pose

In solitary meditation
　　fingertips to palm
　　ankle around calf
　　she invites his image—
　　　a cerebral genie.

Oh! The mystical man
whose love beads lure her…
　　Yet six lunar cycles
　　　　alone
　　cannot tempt her
　　　to bridge
　　the fantasy.

Her gaze soft and fixed
　　her core centered
　　her body open
　　　to reality—
　　she closes
　her practiced mind.

First Date

Slightly out of tune,
I tilt on a hardwood chair
beside a gentleman friend
in a pub of tapping tables
where the singer rasps a chorus
about his hesitation blues while
I cross, uncross, recross my legs,
clasping my ringless fingers
like unfamiliar frets, spying
behind, between, finally past
a woman in a brown satin blouse
and her lover gently strumming
the curve of her scapula,
as the guitarist sings of
a rainbow over his shoulder
that shines like gold—
an Aegean weave of words
upon which I make a wish.

The Trouble with Troubadours

The Irish poet strode
stage left through the entrance
of the desanctified church
as the piano player crooned
"It's Been A Long Long Time"—
inviting kisses upon kisses….
And, oh, was it my imagining?
That in a glance (and was that a wink?)
that I knew this Bard and I
had loved each other in a past life
in a house in the Irish countryside—
with every sharp corner
lovingly filled and smoothed
so no Evil Spirits might lurk—
in a house where we rose winter after winter
sound beneath its thatched roof through which
neither the bite of frost nor the damp of tears
could ever penetrate.
As he held his sheaves of poetry in one hand,
then tousled his hair with the other,
I willed his breath along the slope of my neck…
where he lingered long over
one fine and lusty love poem—
undoubtedly written
just for me.

Parlay

Streamsong rose
like morning mist
Dickinsonian ribbons
fanlike within
where breath inspires

like the surge
of sap conveying
through a sturdy sapling
the confidence that now
is a tree at ease

La Seduzione

Luglio (July) 1998

Of all the fruits—
melon wrapped
in marbled prosciutto,
sliced grapes carried
from the *alimentari,*
pearl-like berries
(desired yet untaken)
        —it was the nectarine,
        his description of
        the nectarine,
        its ripeness,
        its velvety skin,
        its testicular shape,
        which aroused her *appetito*
        on the *ristorante* balcony in
        the blessed *porto* of Assisi.

Perugian Pear

Perugian
Pear
To call it
simply a drupe,
the botanical label
bestowed upon stone fruits,
is to know neither the vision of
its triple layers of skin, stone, & flesh,
nor the hidden kernel at the center of this
alabaster pear graced by one verdigris leaf
with polished streaks its loving sculptor
would refer to as "stains of berry blue,"
nor as an object of art presented
sweetly by its object of
affection.

Dawn

the accomplice of love is art folded in a paper fortune revealing unlocked luggage yawns images like mist on that lake inside moss woods below silver rivets through jet wings clouds feathery quills inked by stars burst sunflowers peak through shutters above the alley of rain pearls one cobbled roadway drawing beyond the train cars toward terracotta warriors on guard for hearts in hidden rooms where mourning love breaks smooth scented linens sigh their finale...

aubade aubade aubade

The Antidote to Love

I prescribed you as my anesthesia—
so long as you treated me as elixir.
Like coveted fluid in amber glass,

I scripted you to hold me to the Light—
so long as my essence remain unshattered.
Oh, for the power to conjure, to slip into

wizard robes, to steal alchemists' secrets,
to sedate our stricken souls having
chosen Lust as the antidote to Love.

I envisioned our crushed spirits released like
vapors escaping from an apothecary bottle.
To recover each self would be the cure.

Restored, all I asked, was for you to recall me
as one might a cherished memento mori
and that I was a treasure once.

The Tending

On a hearth of hearts,
love emblazoned by
sparks jealously contained
by blackened firebricks,
we built fires over and again,
consumed by the knowledge
that flames flicker best above
a bed of ashes from spent blazes.
Like all lovers seasoned by time,
we were once kindled by a single illumination—
even an eternal flame requires keepers.

Hesitation Waltz

The ghazal completed, the poet stumbles upon two lines:
True ease in writing comes from art, not chance,
As those move easiest who have learned to dance.
—Alexander Pope

The two step up to the dance to take a chance—
tempted, no, compelled to take a chance—

as if to a French minuet, each sways gracefully,
one bows, one curtsies to enhance the chance

of brushing fingertips before spinning apart. Or,
at second glance, was their touch only by chance?

Under spiky stars, welcoming right romance
to be likers and lovers amazed for the chance,

the couple awakens each celestial dancer within
by twirling round in a daring dance of chance—

risking demise like medieval sword dancers, or perchance
miming in Marriage Dance like Cubans would chance,

or Hesitation Waltzing by well-heeled Americans, or
Becoming One with God as Persians hope to chance.

Or will each partner feign confidence to glide side by side,
yet stumble lock-stepped in their stance of last chance?

Is love a grand plan or cosmic happenstance?
Oh, for the brief caress, for the sole fleeting chance,

for sparkling in the night—as if by candle Rumi lights
for sharing the bold bliss of chancing a chance.

II.

Riptide

You must do the thing you think you cannot do.

—Eleanor Roosevelt

Every Poet's Heart's Desire

Every poet's Heart's desire
Is each Truth told—that we Aspire—

Long we to be so gladly Dead
With not one buried Word unsaid—

Pray not our thoughts Wild remain—
Save ones found in the Public Domain

The Triangle

My ten-year-long legs dangle
from a bench painted
Parks Department green.
Gingerly I perch
to avoid splinters
from knife-whittled slats
where TK luvs LM 4 ever.
I peer beyond our boulevard
to a vanishing point—
a distant land beckoning
this Whitestone girl as
the cream and green Q16
lurches along the roadway.
I leap from the seat
on a triangle of curbs
to hug a shaved neck
in a pressed white shirt
home from the island city.

In the Audience 1962

1

On the carpeted dais inside
Castel Gandolfo in Italia,
I am a wide-eyed child.
I see cheering crowds surge
behind wooden gated corrals
as Swiss Guards pose and
preen in satin and plumes.

Among the selected seated,
my Catholic family waits.
Regal robes of holy fathers
and mothers superior swoosh
past our red velvet benches.
We peer down upon pilgrims
making the sign of the cross.

Pope John XXIII arrives
elevated on a golden chair!
The trumpets! The banners!
Vive le Pape! *Vive le Pape!*
Long live the Pope!
With a gesture of his hand,
we are hushed....

2

Home in America, I await,
like Bernadette of Lourdes,
for an image to descend.
I implore with all my might:

Grant the gift of Grace to me!
Grant the gift of Faith to me!

Decades on, an image does descend:
I am one closed-eyed old woman,
palms extended and uplifted,
kneeling, fading, waiting
for my blessing yet
to be bestowed.

Peppermint Twist Politics 1962

The moment [that] a feeling enters the body is political.
—Adrienne Rich, journal entry

Girls in dresses, boys in suits and ties
danced to the latest craze—the Twist.
That spring, in the United States,
I was a pre-teen mesmerized
by TV's *American Bandstand*

That summer in Europe, we crossed
the border to Grandma's hometown
birthplace in the Republic of Austria
where oompah bands keep ¾ time.
A post warned: TWIST VERBOTEN!

Beneath alpine stars, that evening,
girls in dirndls, boys in lederhosen
spun in pairs but split to twist
when the clarinet brassily broke
into a Chubby Checker tune.

That moment, I sat stunned
on the metal biergarten chair;
my childhood short-circuited;
my thoughts skittered: *No! Stop!*
Why would they...? Then...Why not?

Black-capped, white-shirted *polizei*
led the teen rebels into the shadows.
Town elders rushed the dance floor
and the accordion burst out a polka.
We were in the Old Country, that night.

My Silenced Spring

A Call to Mind: 1970-2020
Oh, when will they ever learn?
      —Pete Seeger

April 22, 1970

What do we want? / Clean air!
      On that first Earth Day, with my high school friends, I skipped down subway steps (Flushing's Main Street station), the mission to save the nation from the General of Motors, who had yet to drum out loyalists to Rachel Carson's warnings of future songless mornings. White surgical masks donned, our pea coats from the Army & Navy store buttoned down, up the stairwell we charged. We paraded past barricades out of line, giddy & fearless in our freedom to chant:

What do we want? / Clean air!
      When do we want it? / Now!

May 4, 1970

What do we want? / Peace!
      Bared bayonetted rifles aimed to halt our college students with civil rights to assemble. Without warning, Guardsmen of our Nation, who never intended to kill their fellow American citizens, randomly struck down protestors and passersby. Speakers against war sprawled on the ground felled by bullets. States away, in my parochial uniform, I disassembled. Too shattered to wield my will, too numb to cry out:

What did we want? / Peace.
      When did we want it? / Then.

Thirty-Odd Degrees

Warming my rump on the steamy hood
of a '68 Caddy late January '77,
I tilt my head to let the sun feel

my face which rests on hands which rest
on the handle of a hand-me-down shovel.
For one city moment—no cars, trucks, or buses,

no crunch, chop or scrape—just profound
quiet. Today I am a lucky soul.
Windless winter warms me as

icicles plummet, gutter water trickles
in a blazing forenoon sun.
Knuckles pound an aluminum storm door.

A single-engine plane rumbles overhead.
Then…mighty silence.
The sound of my own breath humbles me.

Boots sliding from the front bumper
I unstraddle the shovel and loosen
the jacket from my balmy body.

Personal Effects 1987

Tears are heart vapors that rise to the head and escape.
—17th century folklore

I will see one man die twice.
A black man who hues blue
as I spoon-feed my sheet-white father
yellow mash in his VA hospital room.
The first time the gentleman dies
he is sitting up. Legs hung
over the rumpled linens,
he tugs at the tube taped
to his nostril. A figure glides
past the doorway, asks
the peppery-haired fellow
how he's doing, and he gurgles
"Ohh-kuh-kuh-kaay..."
Uplifted in greeting, his arm
ratchets, he keels backward.
"He's not breathing!" I gasp
to the desk nurse who sighs,
clicks her ballpoint pen closed,
trudges in but bolts out
shouting a code that's blue too.

The next Sunday, I smooth
the withered stroke-clenched hand
of my blind unblinking father,
convinced he knows nothing
of the blue balloon of a man
who seems mummified in taut
creaseless sheets stamped
with the Castle Point imprint
when an electronic screech summons

a team of starch-white uniforms.
In slow code mode, personnel
defibrillate, disconnect, detach:
"Who's got the personal effects bag?"
I spoon-feed my father green mash until
he seals his lips, squeezes his eyelids shut.
One tear escapes, and I know he knows.

Riptide

Show me
the poetry
in pregnancy:
Your placenta settled
like a creature sunken—one
heartbeat from hemorrhage.
You, a tiny survivor,
floated shut-eyed,
suspended
in love's
riptide.

Veterans Administration Hospital Guidelines for Laundry Attendants

A hospital and an outside laundry service should work closely together to improve linen management.

—NIH.gov

Whose hand first sorted the soiled material,
kept the proper linen distribution log,
pulled open the hopper discharge door?

Whose hand tossed the dried sheets
to a cart on the scale, switched on
the finishing and folding machines?

Whose hand stacked the linens
lifted onto rolling racks then
steered to my hospital room?

Whose hand guided those bedsheets
with the Veterans Hospital's imprint
onto the mattress of my maternity bed?

I watch the fabric float through the air,
smoothed, tucked, cornered, when I gasp,
"Castle Point! My Dad died there!"

"I'll take them off," cries the aide.
"No! Don't!" Then I assure her:
"It's a message from my father."

Oh, could I doubt the news of my
near death and baby's rush baptism
would be delivered by whose hand?

The Turnaround

1

You, my daughter,
blaze your path
four wheels level
on spears of grass.

2

My engine killed,
you query my delay,
ask first time ever,
Are *you* okay?

My American Star Quilt

somewhere in the unknown world / a yellow eyed woman/
sits with her daughter / quilting

—Lucille Clifton

my star quilt   outstretched across my car's hood
another   yard sale   another   letting go
another home to pack up   releasing   once again
when a young mother with two little ones claims
her church is collecting blankets   for victims
of Hurricane Katrina   in New Orleans, Louisiana

I'd handsewn bias tape   to make loops to hang it
too perfect, too precious   to use as a blanket
I think back   to the summer day   I first held it
a hundred dollars saved to buy post-baby clothes
instead I turned back   to the upscale shop
in Bridgehampton   east of the Indian reservation

Stitched by   Native American tribeswomen
a platinumed saleswoman   took pride in telling
wrapping it   in layers   of aqua tissue paper
as if it might break   Yes, please take it, I say
to the young mother   a yellow eyed woman
teaching me   my quilt was never mine   to keep

The Link to Lakes Road

I sometimes steer the curves
on the road 'round Walton Lake
where my Irish grandparents
once owned a weekend place.
Summers, Dad drove us kids
back in his '55 Plymouth—
an aqua and black Belvedere,
Italian for a beautiful view.

Up the road named Heaton,
high ground in Old English,
then down and around, we cruised
past his prewar stomping grounds.
From the American Legion hall,
he'd recall where he, his gal,
and ol' gang dove the waters.
Pretending to see what he saw,
I gazed across the reflections.

Did I inherit his penchant
for the Celtic melancholia?
I picture generations before altars,
their Communions, their Penances.
I hear prayers to lift the English boot
from their broken-spirited necks.
I learn of each passage leaving
Longford, Gaelic for fortress,
to reach a liberated America.

So much of our history a mystery,
the science of genetics reveals
my immigrant grandparents
all-Irish...were part-English.
Was it by free will...or by force?

I swerve, I shudder, at this
question of my heart's ache
I long to forsake each time
I am drawn to steer the curves
on the road 'round Walton Lake.

A Matter of Public Record 1913-1921

We were Irish Republican Army.
'Twas a family secret, it was.

[Condensed from: War of Independence Witness Statements; Signed by poet's
great uncle Michael Francis Heslin; Source: BMH, Military Archives, Ireland]

1

At my father's fireside, I heard from the old Nationalists
of the contingents—armed only with hazel sticks—ready
to drive "the Bullocks" from the Land. As a boy, I witnessed
the R.I.C.—batons drawn and bayonets fixed—impressing
upon me that the Royal Crown indeed was an oppressor of Ireland.

The saddest day in my life would come in the early days
of the troubled period, when I arrived at my father's home
in Cloontumpher to find him and the other old men weeping—
his Killoe Branch United League flag ripped to pieces
by bayonets wielded by both the R.I.C. and the Black and Tans.

2

I, Michael Francis Heslin, an Irish Volunteer joined the I.R.A.
After one hair-raising munitions run from Dublin to Longford,
as Brigade Adjutant and Michael Collins' Intelligence Agent,
I felt the urge to join the fighting forces. Collins directed me
(near threatened me) to stick to "my gun"—my typewriter.

Feigning loyalty to the King, I formed a First-Aid Unit,
organized secret services, studied shorthand writing, and
learned to decode the enemy's telegrams and cypher wires.
Unsealing and resealing British military documents
was brought to a fine art in the Longford Post Office.

The day came when British forces were searching for me.
A lovely woman pedaled twelve miles to give warning.
Two days later came the Truce. I married that brave woman.
To each soul who died to free Ireland, I pay you a tribute.
When I am dead and gone, I am told my story will be told.

Naturalization 1921

For Josef "Pepi" Wurmitzer

He arrived from Austria speaking *Deutsche,*
Italienisch, bisschen Englisch, with barber skills
honed on the heads and chins of the newly deceased.

We American *Enkelkinder* carefully handle
the aged Certificate of Citizenship creased into
eight exact rectangles folded to fit inside his wallet.

We grandchildren question, *why* would he open and
close it so often that it was cellophane taped together.
To keep it intact? Or maybe save him from falling apart.

We learn of Nativists and the laws passed restricting
"undesirables" like the multi-lingual anarchists behind
the infamous still unsolved 1920 Wall Street bombing.

He clipped five hundred feet away at 60 Beaver Street.
We debate: Did he present his paper out of pure pride?
Or, to prove he really was a citizen over and over and....

Mein Gott! Let me rest in peace!
Didn't your Mutter teach you not to
look for trouble—because you will find it?

My Free Spirit Vacation

America! America!
God shed His grace on thee
And crown thy good with brotherhood...
—From "America the Beautiful,' a poem by Katherine Lee Bates

Our shiny charter bus sways
in Bryce Canyon's last light rays
where hoodoo spires guard Ute lands.

We Mericans unload single file
with an old chap in a cap a bit gritty
that claims his *Sun City Is Fun City!*

"I like your hat!" I declare.
"Where you all from?" He stares.
"New York." I flash a Broadway smile.

"Noo Yawk," he parrots, "Noo Yawk."
No cause or pause, the bent man spews:
"Them Noo Yawk Jews have *strange* ideas."

Then with one thrust, the hunched man
worms his fingers into my collarbone,
snarls: "Now you git away from me!"

Hood sliding from my tinted auburn hair,
I sputter, "How do you know *I'm* not Jewish?"
"How? *How?* You got the *wrong* hair color!"

And crown thy good with brotherhood...
God shed His grace on thee
America! America?

55

In the Year Twenty Twenty

Who Lives, Who Dies, Who Tells Your Story
—Lin-Manuel Miranda, lyrics from "Hamilton"

Twenty-fourth of April. Pandemic waves of death, anthem waves of grain, flag waves at half-mast. Fifty thousand dead across our United States. Five thousand in the City of New York. "Victims of Coronavirus die by slow suffocation." Need a mayor say more? "Co" of the Latin *corona,* "Vi" of *virus,* the "D" of *disease—*Covid is coined. And the *19?* For the year. The protocol? *Stay home to save lives.* We hear, but do we heed?

One hundred years ago, the second wave of the Spanish Influenza ebbs. Six hundred seventy-five thousand dead. A year earlier, thirty-year-old Rosa gives birth at home to baby Erna. Newspapers read: How to prevent influenza? *Stay home.*

Two hundred forty-five years ago, Patrick Henry's plea "Give me liberty or give me death!" delivered troops for war against tyranny. Today, so she can party hearty, a twenty-something's sign demands: "Give me Liberty, or Give me Covid!" Middle-aged passengers in a sports utility vehicle protest for their "Freedom from Quarantine!"

Henry supported the speedy and secret inoculation of Revolutionary War troops, ordered by George Washington who wrote that smallpox is "more destructive to an Army in the Natural way, than the Enemy's Sword."

In a Tiananmen moment, one American in hospital scrubs faces down self-appointed patriots. Then the leader of the free world sarcastically suggests subjects self-inject with disinfectant. Conspirators troll, has the fearless one already gotten the vaccine?

Daughter of Erna self-isolates forty days. Biblical tale of Noah to save the believers, two by two. A daily virtual horoscope assures her that "Romance is in the air." She tightens her mask before stepping out into the wind.

Striking Poems

Work is love made visible.
　　　　—Kahlil Gibran

She sees panhandlers with signs

That read Will Work for Food

And wonders, do they mean

To say, Will work for Love?

Her ancestors forged on—

Struck sparks as blacksmiths,

Forced metal with hammers,

Clawed to pull out nailheads,

Slid strike plates to sew clothes,

Held stitch rippers to start over.

Sacrificed selves for love of other.

Their granddaughter, destined too

To rise up, silently writes down—

Scribbles in print, scripts on paper,

Clacks typewriter keys into letters,

Saves words linked to hard drives,

Struggles to chisel fine lines—

Struck by the mettle and hearts

Of those who labored before and

Watch her work at striking poems.

III.

Glossophobia

Speak your mind even if your voice shakes.

—Maggie Kuhn

Heaven's Edge

A barrier of
evergreen steeples
reaches for
the realm of God
who believers
say reigns
in the howling
ashen sky.

Waltz of the Flowers

Since autumn, the Saint Luke's first-grade girls rehearsed
after being led in line, two by two, one finger on lips,
to the convent of the Dominican nuns who taught us.
We seven-year-olds clomped down the wooden stairs
where mysterious white linen shapes floated amidst
black fabric wings hung from laundry lines.

In the cold concrete cellar I struggled to master
the dance routine. Slack knee-high socks,
a thin navy-blue sweater over a short-sleeved blouse,
and my uniform jumper offered little protection
from the damp. "All together now…
Shuffle one, shuffle two. Point one, point two."

That spring, taking my place on the church stage—
crowned with a wire headband of green leaves,
the itch of netting around my waist,
the pull of hairpins against my scalp,
the lipstick on my mouth—I missed the cue,
and lagged two steps behind until the song's end.

Like a pointless prayer, I repeated, "Shuffle one, shuffle two."
As the perfect row of dancing flowers swayed toward the field
of faces, I withered in the opposite direction—my back to pews.
Titters, chuckles, and guffaws escalated into shrieks of hilarity.
I would recall but a silence—as if repeatedly replaying
a grainy old movie with the mute button on.

Afterward my father arrived backstage, wiping away
his own tears of laughter. Did I cry? Did he comfort me?
My perpetual penance for stepping out of line
would be paralysis whenever all eyes turned on me.
Only once did my mother mention that day:
"You were the star of the show."

No Act of Contrition

In stolen moments
        I sit on my chair solely to stare into my past...

We were three Catholic camp counselors when I wished aloud
        to rescue the chair abandoned below the dangling bulb
        in an outbuilding campers used to change for swimming.

Paint-spattered, its leather seat tattered, surely I could redeem it
        from its state of disgrace, and with my unwavering faith
        I would strip it bare and provide perpetual care.

Driving along the camp's edge, my pair of summer friends
        shouted, "Stop!" Climbing over the fence, they broke
        through a hedge, then reappeared, chair hoisted overhead.

It was the thrill of the take—a venial prank; yet
        also a chance to save a soul—a mortal concept
        as if I could miraculously raise Lazarus from the dead.

Gathering sandpaper, varnish stripper, quadruple O steel wool,
        lifting cowhide and horsehair away, I pondered,
        Could this restoration be my eternal condemnation?

I envision the haloed trio I will ask for pardon—
        a boy apprentice who treadled the lathe,
        a woodworker who tooled the fleur-de-lis,
        a genteel woman joyfully accepting delivery.

My golden oak chair with its carved back and turned legs
        poses piously yet warily in the guest room
        where even today it still remains coveted.

Independence Day 1976

On my parents' new balcony
overlooking the garage rooftops,
I slump in a chair, one eye closed,
my legs crossed at the ankles.

There is no sky—
a flat, heavy gray ceiling
rebounds all sound to the ground.

A bird calls to my left;
one on the right returns
the signal in stereo.

Fireworks.
Applause, cheers, then silence.
From the patio below:
laughter, then a lull until
a conversation of soft *s*'s rises.

More fireworks like radio static.
I twist the band on my ring finger
round and round as I descend
the circular stairway to
engage in pointless talk,

I escape to the balcony.
How old will I be
when I say what I mean?

Confessions of a Homeowner

For as long as she lived in the house
she never told a single soul...

The high-heeled agent had ushered them
into the half-brick corner lot Tudor,
for sale by a newly remarried widow.

Evergreen velvet-flocked fleur-de-lis
crept along the walls, up the stairwell,
down the hallway to a master bedroom
featuring twin beds typical of censured
old Hollywood's Hays Code era.
Is this where the husband passed?

With sure steps down squeaky stairs,
the saleswoman pitched the property's
possibilities. The young wife lagged,
alone in the lived-in living room when
then, like a scene from a '50s TV show,
a boy, a girl, a dog buoyantly tumbled
up the stairs, fading into sunlit dust.

The day the house keys passed over,
a hidden panel in the laundry room
revealed a rusty cup hook suspending
a dog leash by its cracked leather strap.
"Kids?" said the neighbor. "The owners
had a son, daughter. Oh, and a mutt too."

Even after moving out, moving on,
she never told a single soul...
of skeletons of her own she left behind.

Oranges & Marigolds

I insist, when ordering funeral flowers—
no yellows, oranges, never ever reds.

Yet, reluctantly, I hold a dead painter's
still life offered heartlessly by his daughter.

I loathe the ragged backsides
of the decayed marigold petals.

I abhor the bloody smears
on the pocked skins of citrus.

I detest its crumbling globs
of carotene and flame crimson.

"Take it," she insisted.
"Take it. Just *take* it!"

And that's what I did.

The Relief

I do not like to write.
I like having written.
    —William Zinsser

So, you may ask:
When is my best time
to write? So, I say,
When is the time best
to pluck out one's thorns?
For two or three hours
I hunch over,
apply drawing salve,
dislodge barbs,
extract shards,
recreate splintered scenes
deeply embedded,
tweeze thoughts
word by word
slowly slowly
until
my eye sockets
demand mercy.

Cabin Fever

Yes! Blue fingers in sweet leather
and a best blouse will thaw me.
Our headlight beams shine on
white & brown Guernseys & Jerseys.
Road signs flare up then leap from view.
Emerald happy-faced tolls flash: *Go! Go!*
High heat blasts from the dash.
Cruise me to The City!

Not soon enough, we bridge
onto the West Side Highway
beckoning like yellow brick.
Anchored pearl ropes shimmer
and trim the Hudson pier-to-pier.
A black & white flashes & screeches
past the docked *USS Intrepid.*
A cold street hawker holds
a hot Sony high. We armor
with tempered glass. Lock! Lock!

A fleeting fix of Manhattan
Manhattans and tenderloin lingers.
Yet, too soon, recrossing county lines,
reflective mailboxes mimic deer in
headlights. Stations hiss static along
back roads where I brace myself against
a blizzard of blues. I reglove my fingers,
and, for a sole second, shiver no more.

Written in Steam

Make visible what, without you,
might perhaps never have been seen.
          —Robert Bresson

With a dull pencil
from the medicine chest,
I scribble sound bites
for pretend listeners
as the shower water
whistles cold to hot.
Is this my so-called spare time?

Agatha Christie plotted
murders while washing
dishes, then sprinkled
red herrings while
soaking in her tub.
When do I have time to take a bath?

I sweat over the
volunteer minutes.
It is the dry writing
that makes me thirsty.
When do I get to be a good cause?

Our laundry, crushed,
tumbled, un-pressed,
lazes on the sofa.
It is the repetition,
the refrain of do-over,
the invisible work
that drains me.
Wash, fold, put away, wash, fold,

away, away....
Until I ignore
the chore lists,
the cracked tile walls,
the invisible becomes visible,
the visible becomes audible
when I read my words aloud
as the shower water
whistles cold to hot.

Turning Forty

Turning
forty on
a full moon.
Let the lunacy
begin.

Dream Dirge

Asleep on a field of stones,
she spoons 'round her girl-child
when daybreak hammers a chasm
across her salted sealed eyelids.

Feathers sheening from toxic waste,
a raven punctures her neck with its beak:
Something—or someone—will die.

Not *her* child, she swears.
And in one swoop, cocooning
the girl with her cloak, she
chokes the tormentor to death.

Making the Cut

Joy is not made to be a crumb.
    —Mary Oliver

The air a sea of creatures—
horseflies and zigzagging birds—
clipping crisscross glinting electric
wires that skip rope with the sun.

The scent of sappy evergreen
engages my sense of seasons to come
while I sip coffee iced, and the sunlight
simmers on my polished toes.

Treasure the memory of this day against
the underside of the fall before winter's
hurry-to-the-door-don't-let-the-cold-in
days for sure on their way.

No, no, no—*no one*
can steal this surge from me
to stop the bloodletting
and start my healing.

Secret Epistle

You'll always be my friend.
You know too much.
      —Magnet once gifted

In the split blink you saw
that louse of an in-law

molest my breast,
you begged don't protest

with your deer-eyed look,
stunned but not too shook

to protect yourself.
I'd neglect myself

become complicit
our future implicit.

Each silenced voice
each certain choice

to keep the secret to our end—
to lose the best of a friend.

How do *you* measure the silence?

I calculate the loss
each calendar I cross.

Show of Mercy: A Lament

As the news breaks, the Bishop of Rome
declares 2016 to be "The Year of Mercy"

With consecrated virgins at his call,
Benedict XVI conveniently uninstalled
then retired behind Vatican convent walls.

He has lost his spiritual strength, they say,
as one means to keep him out of the way;
his sole function as Pope Emeritus is to pray.

While in hiding, *arresti domiciliari* conceals
the past perfect padre who piously kneels
harbored in perpetual exile that shields.

His papal fisherman's ring torched by fire,
wearing white since on ice, does he conspire
with his sure hell to freeze afore he expires?

Cloistered and contained as keeper of the gall,
he secretes that brothers tall hurt brothers small.
(The cruelest twist on brotherly love for all.)

Bending, the See's obedient followers turn deaf ears
to claims of his brother's choir cruelty for years.
For when the smoke from censers disappears,
                                        Let him pray.

Trataka

A Gazing Meditation

The moon is not always what it is cracked up to be,
one fractured crescent fingernail tip sheared at its nail bed—

I'll sit tonight, wallow in my misery and ready the pity party
for those dramas and tragedies conjured in my head—

I INTERRUPT THIS RUMINATION FOR A BULLETIN

BREAKING WITH LOOPS OF AUDIO OF MORE RAPID

GUNFIRE BURSTING FROM MASS MURDER MUZZLES

IN OUR UNTIED STATES. AND WE NOW RETURN TO A

PAINFULLY HOLLOW POEM CURRENTLY IN PROGRESS.

A red moon wanes, entrance wounds gape, exit wounds bleed out,
chests suck air, organs spill forth, my third eye implodes—

Oh, I'll sit tonight, cancel my pity party, and suffer the misery
of selfish shame and endless grief that riddles my head—

Burning Bowl Ceremony

Remember, the entrance door
to the sanctuary is inside you.
                                    —Rumi

In a place of new thought, on
an elevated table, a blown glass
bowl awaits
                    my ashes of anguish.
Congregants pen the burning matter
each desires to release by setting
virtual bonfires of lightness.
                                        I too
long to douse loss, snuff disbelief.
Have I the willingness to experiment?
Can I repair despair with good intention?
Calculated chemistry? Or simple science?
Is a wish the same
                    as a prayer?
Each torched square of flash paper
combusts midair with a *whoosh!*
All except mine.
                    The browning edge
of dried parchment resists ignition.
Unable to bear the intensity any longer,
I drop the still-flaming matchstick.
My inked words
                    sink then smolder
into carbon curls of crackling black
when a new thought arises sparking
a refrain on which I meditate:
To extinguish ...
                    I must relinquish.

The Translation

You are going to pierce infinity!
—Juan Felipe Herrera

The translation
of my drawing
requires words
to mark markings
on bone-leather
cockled parchment.
Writing tight
on folded paper
recalls Wearever
script on feathery
airmail letters;
I have no language
to explain inexplicable.
Concentrate:
translate, relate,
calculate, collate,
contemplate, manipulate,
devastate, mutilate.
Our poet teacher schools:
"Question marks are loud!"
Sounds on the page:
tapping of instruments,
racket on wood,
minds penning.
But who will unfold
the parchment
to hear me?

Notes

Katherine Lee Bates (b. 1859) American writer, social activist.
Bishop of Rome (b. 1936) Less formal title Pope Francis prefers.
Robert Bresson (b. 1901) French artist, writer, and film director.
Rachel Carson (b. 1907) American marine biologist, author, conservationist.
Lucille Clifton (b.1936) American writer, educator, and poet.
Kahlil Gibran (b. 1883) Lebanese American poet.
Seamus Heaney (b. 1939) Irish poet, playwright, translator, winner of the Noble Prize in Literature.
Juan Felipe Herrera (b. 1948) Performer, writer, cartoonist, teacher, activist, Twenty-first United States Poet Laureate.
Maggie Kuhn (b. 1905) American activist.
Lin-Manuel Miranda (b. 1980) American composer, lyricist, actor.
Mary Oliver (b. 1935) American poet, winner of the Pulitzer Prize and the National Book Award.
Alexander Pope (b. 1688) English poet.
Adrienne Rich (b. 1929) American poet, essayist, feminist.
Eleanor Roosevelt (b. 1884) American political figure and activist.
Rumi (b. 1207) Persian poet, scholar, lawyer, theologian.
Pete Seeger (b. 1919) American folksinger, songwriter, and political activist.
Carl Yung (b. 1875) Swiss psychologist and psychiatrist.
William Zinsser (b. 1922) American writer, critic, and teacher.

"Walk on air against your better judgement" is Seamus Heaney's headstone epitaph, a line from his poem "The Gravel Walks."

I.R.A. The Irish Republican Army.
R.I.C. The Royal Irish Constabulary.
Black and Tans. Royal Irish Constabulary reinforcements.
BMH (The Bureau of Military History). To search this source online, go to: www.militaryarchives.ie., All Collections, The Bureau of Military History, 1913-1921.

About the Author

Mary Louise Kiernan is the grateful recipient of two literary honors: the Walt Whitman Award for Excellence in Creative Writing from Queensborough Community College and a 2015 Poetry Prize from Tempe Public Library and Arizona State University. Her first laurel baffled, the second emboldened.

In addition to the poems listed on the Acknowledgments page, her essays have been published in *The Times Herald-Record, Catskill Country Magazine,* and *The New York Times.* Indeed, one (multiply rejected) first-person essay on glossophobia planted the seed for her poem "The Waltz of the Flowers."

Mary Louise Kiernan holds her Bachelor of Arts degree in Communications in Written Media from SUNY Empire State College, where she studied under Mary Makofske.

Poetry writing workshops have been at the core of Mary Louise Kiernan's education. Some workshops attended include: *Finding Our Voices: Women and Creativity,* at SUNY Orange Campus, with the late Lucille Clifton; The Omega Institute, with Sharon Olds; The New York State Writers Institute, with Peg Boyers, with a critique by Barry Goldensohn, at Skidmore College; the 2016 Sunken Garden Poetry Festival, with past U.S. Poet Laureate Juan Felipe Herrera; the Poets House, with Nickole Brown and Jessica Jacobs; and a SUNY Master Class Workshop, with Molly Peacock.

Up-to-date information may be found at marylouisekiernan.com.

www.ingramcontent.com/pod-product-compliance
Lightning Source LLC
Chambersburg PA
CBHW072046090426
42733CB00032B/2360